Leader's Guide

When
CHRIST
Lives
in
Us

A Pilgrimage of Faith

Justo L. González

Abingdon Press
NASHVILLE

WHEN CHRIST LIVES IN US
Leader's Guide

by Justo L. González

Copyright © 1996 by Abingdon Press

ISBN: 0-687-01562-6

William A. Woods, Designer

Abingdon Press

CONTENTS

Introduction

The book *When Christ Lives in Us* may be read either in private or in a number of group settings. Individual readers do not need a study guide beyond what is suggested at the end of the introduction to the book. Those who plan to use *When Christ Lives in Us* in group settings, however, may wish to have ideas and suggestions as to how to present the book, as to what activities may help a group understand what the book says, and so forth. This Leader's Guide is intended to provide such help. It should not be used as a substitute for the book itself, however; for it has very little content per se and dwells mostly on methods and activities. Also, teachers, pastors, and others planning to lead a group through the study of the book are strongly encouraged to read *When Christ Lives in Us* in its entirety before the study begins in order to have a fuller view of the general direction of the book and the thrust of its argument.

Several different settings and uses are discussed in the pages that follow. Part I presupposes study sessions of up to two-and-a-half hours on each chapter of the book. The first five chapters of that section may be used for adult vacation Bible school and are planned with that setting in mind. Part II includes suggestions and outlines for use in Sunday school classes—normally at the rate of a chapter each class, but also with some suggestions for studying the book in a month and for extending the study over a quarter. Parts III, IV, and V deal with more specific settings: retreats, stewardship studies, and membership classes, respectively.

Since some activities are suggested for more than one of these settings, it has been necessary to cross-reference this Leader's Guide in order to avoid needless repetition. Thus, under Part II you may find a suggestion: "See **Part I, Chapter 2, F.**" I realize that this may be confusing for the leader planning a session, and I apologize for the inconvenience it may cause. It may, however, have one value: It may encourage you to look at other parts of the book and to use your own creativity in combining suggestions from various sections. If so, the value gained may well be worth the aggravation!

Part I

Use in Small Groups and Vacation Bible School

One possible setting for the study of *When Christ Lives in Us* is small groups meeting for sessions of up to two-and-a-half hours. Since adult vacation Bible school classes often meet for such periods, sometimes in the evenings, they provide an ideal opportunity for such study.

Small groups meeting for fewer than eight sessions, whether VBS classes or other groups, may choose to study only certain chapters of *When Christ Lives in Us*. If such is the case in your group, encourage members to read the remaining chapters individually. However, as the book emphasizes the need that we have of one another in order to grow in Christ, stress the importance of group members making a covenant to continue their mutual support and prayer, no matter whether their study continues as a group or as individuals.

When the study program is announced, make certain that all those planning to attend have a copy of *When Christ Lives in Us*. Tell them that for the first session they should read the Introduction as well as the first chapter. If you do not do this, the class session will be spent in repeating what the book says for those who have not read it. Once that pattern is established, some people will decide that they do not have to come to the class sessions because they can just as well read the book at home; and others will decide that there is no point in reading the book because they will be told what it says when the class meets.

Reading the book and attending the class sessions are complementary, and each builds on the other. While reading at home, participants may take the time to go back over a particular paragraph that is not clear; or they may take a moment for prayer about something that strikes them as they read. They can meditate quietly and privately about the implications for their lives of what they are reading. Then, in the class session, they can help one another discover further dimensions in what they are studying; they can share their discoveries, doubts, and decisions; and they can support one another. Both elements, reading in private and meeting as a class, are equally important; and one should not be substituted for the other.

****

The leader's material for the small group study of *When Christ Lives in Us* is organized by the chapters of the book. For each chapter, a section on preparation indicates what assignments should be made before that session and what materials should be available. It is understood that group members will read the relevant pages in the book prior to the group meeting. (Note that all page numbers in brackets refer to *When Christ Lives in Us*.)

Within the chapter divisions, successive themes are indicated by bold capital letters (**A.**, **B.**, **C.**), successive questions or activities around these themes by bold Arabic numerals (**1.**, **2.**, **3.**), and variations on these questions or activities by bold lowercase letters (**a.**, **b.**, **c.**). Options in method are indicated by **OR**. However, leaders may choose among themes, questions, and activities to customize the session for their group and time frame.

Depending on the size and format of your group, you may wish to have informal introductions and some form of check-in at the beginning of each session.

Chapter 1: Calling [pages 10–20]

Preparation. Have a chalkboard and chalk or a large sheet of paper and a marker available. If you choose to employ the debate option in **B.3**, contact the two debaters several days before the session. For **D.2**, prepare the report on Paul in advance or ask a group member to prepare it. For **E.3**, provide a pen or pencil and a few slips of paper for each group member.

A. Open this session—and every session—with prayer. This is not just an intellectual study; this is an exercise in opening ourselves to God's will. It may change our lives radically. Therefore, it must not be taken lightly.

B. During this session you may wish to spend some time talking about the Introduction [pages 5–9], for it sets the tone for the whole book. By discussing the Introduction, you will help the group understand the purpose of this study and these sessions.

   1. In order to do this, write on a chalkboard or on a large sheet of paper three images that appear in that Introduction: "being in Christ," "Christ formed in us," and "imitation of Christ." Ask group members to comment on what each of these images conveys to them and what they expect to find in a book entitled *When Christ Lives in Us*.

OR

2. Lead the group in a discussion of the values and the shortcomings of the phrase "imitation of Christ" as the central understanding of the Christian life.

OR

3. Several days before the session, ask two members of the group who are articulate and well-spoken to prepare to debate the following proposition: "The basis of the Christian life is the imitation of Christ." One is to argue that this proposition is correct, and the other is to argue that it is wrong or that it is insufficient. If you choose this option, make certain that you select two people who will be able to enter into such a debate without taking it personally. You do not want real animosities to develop!

Tell these two people that the debate will serve as a brief introduction to the entire series of studies. Each debater will have three minutes to develop his or her arguments and then another minute in which to respond to the other's arguments: four minutes for each person, eight minutes total.

When the study group meets, explain that you have asked these two people to debate the proposition as a way to bring to life the issues considered in the Introduction to the book. After the debate, allow a few minutes for discussion among the group; then close that discussion by inviting the group to move on to the subject of Chapter 1.

C. Introduce Chapter 1 by helping the group understand the power of calling and the power of words and names.

1. You may do this by giving opportunity for any who wish to do so to react to the assertion in the book that "before coming into being, all things are pronounced by God and that it is because God pronounces them that they come into being" [pages 10–11]. In such a discussion, make sure that the group refers back to the beginning of Genesis as well as to the beginning of John.

OR

2. You may lead the group in reflecting on what their own names mean to them—as well as the names they give their children. For this activity there are several routes you can select or combine:

   a. Ask if there are any in the group who have chosen to be called by a different name than the one their parents gave them. Invite these persons to comment on why they made that choice and what difference it has made in their lives.

   b. Make a list of names that have particular meanings or connotations (names such as Hope, Faith, Charity, Wesley, Martin Luther, Patience, George Washington, or Napoleon). Ask members of the group to imagine that one of these names is their name. Ask: *Would it make any difference in your life? Why or why not?*

   c. Ask those who are parents to share stories about the process of choosing names for their children. Why was the naming of their children so important? What was at stake?

   OR

3. Ask group members how they think that constantly telling a child, "You are bad" will affect that child's life. Invite them to comment on the value of the old saying that "sticks and stones may break my bones, but words can never hurt me."

   AND/OR

4. If time permits, you may wish to lead the group in a discussion of the following paragraph from a worldwide report on baptism, Eucharist, and ministry:

   In some parts of the world, the giving of a name in the baptismal liturgy has led to confusion between baptism and customs regarding name-giving. This confusion is especially harmful if, in cultures predominantly not Christian, the baptized are required to assume Christian names not rooted in their cultural tradition. . . . A name which is inherited from one's original culture roots the baptized in that culture, and at the same time manifests the universality of baptism.[1]

   After reading, ask questions such as: *What is implied when someone tells a convert from a particular culture that she or he must take a "Christian" (meaning a Western) name? What would be implied in our own culture if a person coming to baptism asked to be given a new name? Would this be a sign*

9

of being born anew, of a radically new beginning? Or would it mean something else?

D. Now turn the attention of the group toward their own calling.

1. Point out that if it is true that nothing comes into being without being called by God (see John 1:3), then it makes no sense to discuss whether we are called by God. No one can say that he or she is *not* called. Our very existence is an act of calling. God has called us to exist, and God certainly has not called us into being for nothing. Our being called into existence is the first of a series of callings whereby God will make us into what we are to be. Indeed, the life of discipleship is a series of callings.

2. To emphasize that the life of discipleship is a series of callings, you may have the group review the life of Paul and see how many times he was called (see Chapters 9, 11, 13, 15, and 16 in Acts, for example). Another approach would be to ask a member of the group to prepare beforehand a short report on this subject or to prepare such a report yourself. (By the way, the common assertion that "Saul" was his name before his conversion and "Paul" was his name afterwards is not true. He had two names, one Hebrew—*Saul*—and one Hellenistic— *Paul*—as was customary among many Jews at the time.)

OR

3. If the group members are comfortable speaking about themselves, ask if any of them wish to give a testimony of how they believe God has called them at different times in their lives.

E. Remind the class that calling always involves a negative side, a renunciation, a leaving something behind.

1. Review with the group what the book says about this point— the need to "travel light" [pages 13–14]—and how things that are perfectly good in some settings may be a hindrance when we undertake a journey.

2. On renunciation, you may wish to read aloud the following paragraph and ask for responses to it:

Today one gets the impression that people become frustrated because they want to be happy at any price. They suffer from frustration anxiety; they think they might miss something, that something might escape them before they have to go; and at the same time they know that soon they must go and there is not much time left in which to find happiness. That is why they take care not to let anything slip by them. But in reality this fear of not being able to consume everything spread out on the table of life means that nothing is enjoyed.

Ask: *Is this an accurate description of modern life? Do you see any relationship between this and what is said in the book about the need to "travel light" and to leave behind those things that are not suitable for the journey? Is it correct to claim that happiness will elude any who seek to lead a full life by grasping at everything?*

3. Now invite the group to consider those things that may be hindrances in their obedience to their calling. Explain clearly that these hindrances do not have to be the same things for everybody and that they depend on one's particular calling. For instance, a medical doctor may well be called to heal the sick where she is; and in that case her practice and career are not a hindrance to her calling. But if that same person is called to be a missionary doctor overseas, then she must leave behind her practice and let her medical career take her elsewhere. And, if she is called to be a preacher, then she may have to leave behind both her practice and her medical career.

Probably the best way to have people consider this concept is to take some time for silent, private meditation. Give each group member a pencil and a few slips of paper, each slip small enough to be easily carried in a wallet. Ask group members to write on each slip of paper, for their own private use only, one of the things that they believe is a hindrance in their pilgrimage of faith. Then tell them to put the slips of paper in their wallets; to keep them there; and to throw each of them away only when (a) they have actually given up whatever the hindrance is, or (b) they have discovered that they were wrong, that the supposed hindrance was not in fact a hindrance.

F. According to the chapter we are studying, although there are a variety of Christian callings, every disciple is called to call others— that is to say, an essential part of Christian discipleship is inviting others to similar discipleship. Ask: *What do you think:* **Is** *every Christian called to invite others to participate in discipleship? Explain your answer.*

G. Conclude the session by telling the group that, although "Calling" is the title of our first chapter, throughout this study we shall be trying to be faithful to our various callings as disciples of Jesus. We shall not press anyone into telling the rest of the group personal secrets or feelings. But at the same time, we must all be open and ready when any of us wishes to share with others how her or his calling is becoming clearer or more difficult in the course of this study.

H. Give opportunity for any who feel the need to share something before the session ends to do so; then dismiss the group with prayer.

---

[1] From *Baptism, Eucharist and Ministry*, Faith and Order Paper No. 111 (World Council of Churches, 1982); page 7.

Chapter 2: Praying [pages 21–31]

Preparation. Have a chalkboard and chalk or a large sheet of paper and a marker available. For the comparison in **E**, have enough NRSV Bibles on hand for each group member to read along. If you wish to relate the parable of the friends to our life of prayer and response to need as in **G**, bring several recent newspapers to class.

A. Open the session with prayer. Then review the previous session. Take no more than fifteen minutes to remind the group of the highlights of that first chapter—especially the point that the life of discipleship is a life of calling and that, although each one of us has a different calling, we are all called to call others to discipleship.

B. Depending on the time available and the interests of your study group, you may wish to spend some time on the first section of the chapter, "Jesus at Prayer" [pages 21–22]. If so, the easiest procedure may be to read aloud one or two selections from the book and invite group members to comment on them.

C. As you move into the section "Teach Us to Pray" [pages 23–27], help the group see the importance of the use of the plural in the Lord's Prayer. In order to do this, you may:

    1. Write on a chalkboard or on a large sheet of paper a version of the Lord's Prayer in the singular ("My Father, who art in heaven . . . give me this day my daily bread . . . forgive me my trespasses," and so forth). Ask: *What difference does that change make?* Then ask: *Why do you think Jesus taught his disciples to pray "Our Father"?*

OR

    2. Ask the group about differences between praying the Lord's Prayer Sunday morning in church and praying it alone at home. When group members say the prayer at church, how do they relate to the rest of the congregation? When they say it at home, do they think in individual terms? How do the words themselves make them think of praying with others?

D. Help the group see the paradox that the book points out between the title "Father" and the phrase "in heaven" [pages 23–24]—or, if you wish to focus only on Luke's version of the prayer, between "Father" and "hallowed be your name." You may do this by using one or both of the following methods:

    1. Review what the book says about the author's mother being the principal of his school when he was a youth [page 25]. Ask group members to tell about similar situations in their own lives (for instance, some may be preacher's kids or may be employed by one of their parents or close relatives). Ask how such situations help them understand the tension and the beauty of being able to call God Almighty "Our Father."

    2. Ask the group to make two lists of words, one that speaks of God's grandeur (omnipotent, majestic, holy, and so forth) and another that speaks of God's closeness to us (father, parent, friend, and so forth). Write the suggestions in parallel columns on a chalkboard or on a large sheet of paper. Ask members of the group which of these lists is more important to them as they pray and why. (Probably both are equally important, for we pray to a powerful God who cares about us.)

E. Explore the meaning of the Lord's Prayer by having the group compare Luke's version with Matthew's (Matthew 6:9-13.) You will need to have enough copies of NRSV Bibles so that each member can read the verses from Matthew. Matthew's prayer is longer. But does it really add anything to Luke's? Or are Matthew's additions implied in Luke's version?

F. Move to the parable of the friends that follows the Lord's Prayer in Luke's Gospel (Luke 11:5-8). Ask someone to read it aloud. Review the analysis of that parable in the book, especially the identification of the three parties as "Friend A," "Friend B," and "Friend C" [pages 27–29]. Have the group explore the following issues:

1. Suppose that Friend B has ample bread in his house when Friend A arrives. Would it be legitimate for him to go knocking at Friend C's door asking for bread? If he does, what would be an appropriate response from Friend C?
2. Suppose that there is no Friend A. Friend B simply feels that baking bread is too difficult and therefore goes to Friend C for bread. What would be an appropriate response from Friend C?
3. Again, suppose there is no Friend A. Friend B has bread. But he would rather have fancier food, so he asks Friend C for caviar and smoked salmon. What would be an appropriate response from Friend C?
4. Or suppose that Friend A comes with bread, and Friend B wants to show off. Again, he goes to Friend C for caviar and smoked salmon. What would be an appropriate response from Friend C?

G. Relate the four options in **F** to our life of prayer and response to need. Help the group explore what all this means for us as Christians when we learn that there is a need and decide to pray for it to be met. Ask: *Are we justified in praying for the need to be met if we ourselves do not do all that we possibly can? Are we justified in praying for expensive cars and fur coats when there is so much hunger in the world? Why or why not?*

1. Bring several recent newspapers to the session and ask group members to find in them needs and situations we ought to pray about. After listing these needs and situations, have the group pick two or three for further consideration.
2. Tell the group that these two or three needs and situations represent Friend A, coming to us in need. Then ask: ***What bread***

or other resources do we have to respond to these needs? Are we justified in praying for these needs if we do not do what we can to meet them with our own resources? What must we do before we go and ask Friend C (God) to meet those needs?

3. Read Luke 6:38, where the phrase appears, "Give, and it will be given to you." Ask: *How does this relate to "Ask, and it will be given you"?*

H. Finally, move to Luke 11:9-13. In the light of the preceding parable of the friends, how are we to understand the phrase, "Ask, and it will be given you"? Are we to ask for just anything? Lead the class in discussing the following questions:
1. What are some reasons *not* to ask for something?
2. Who determines what is *good* for a child?
3. What does the text tell us is the *best* gift from God?

I. In closing, point out to the group that when we ask for the Holy Spirit, we are also asking for the power that will guide us in our further asking. Thus, there is a sort of cycle: We ask for and receive the Holy Spirit, who in turn guides us in our asking.

Then lead the class in a closing prayer.

Chapter 3: Feeding [pages 32–42]

Preparation. Have a chalkboard and chalk or a large sheet of paper and a marker available. For the report suggested in **B.2.a**, several days before the session contact the person you choose to give the report.

Throughout this session it is important to make clear that you are discussing a particular need—hunger—both by way of challenge and by way of example. Various members of the group may decide—or may have decided—to devote their resources to other needs. Your purpose is not to force uniformity of response but to challenge each member of the group to understand this dimension of discipleship and to seek ways to live it out.

A. Open the session with prayer. Then, as this chapter on feeding follows so closely on the previous one on praying, you may wish to begin the session by discussing the relationship between the two.

1. One way of doing this may be by reviewing the parable of the three friends (Luke 11:5-8).
   a. Write on a chalkboard or on a large sheet of paper, next to each other, "Friend A," "Friend B," "Friend C."
   b. Ask the group to recall how these three terms were used in the previous chapter [pages 27–29], in reference to the parable of the unexpected guest and the host who goes to a friend for bread in the middle of the night.
   c. As the discussion unfolds, write under "Friend A" the words "the needy"; under "Friend B," the word "disciple"; and under "Friend C," "God."
   d. Then ask a group member to read aloud the biblical passage for this chapter. As the passage is being read, write "the multitude, "Jesus," and "God" in each of the three columns. At this point, the following should appear on the chalkboard or large sheet of paper:

Friend A	Friend B	Friend C
the needy	disciple	God
the multitude	Jesus	God

   e. Finally, if it seems necessary, ask the group to explain the diagram that has resulted.

   OR

2. Simply have those three columns written on a chalkboard or large sheet of paper before the session begins; briefly review the previous session; and ask members of the group if they can explain the meaning of those three columns, keeping in mind what they have read for this session.

B. The book says that Jesus could have pled two excuses.
   1. First, he could have offered the "spiritual excuse" [pages 33–35]. Ask the group to suggest what they think Jesus could have said in that case.
   2. Second, he could have offered the "purity excuse" [pages 35–36].
      a. Ask someone beforehand to study the laws of purity in ancient Israel. This person could gather information by reading the article "Clean and Unclean" in *The Interpreter's Dictionary of the Bible* (Abingdon, 1962) or by reading a

similar entry in another Bible dictionary. At this point in the session, he or she can report on how Jesus could have pled that excuse. Or, you may read beforehand and make this presentation yourself.

 b. After the report, again ask the group to suggest what Jesus might have said in order to plead this excuse.

 3. An excuse that Jesus could also have given, but which is not mentioned in the book, is "the pragmatic excuse." This amounts to saying that he can do nothing because there just is not enough food, period. Here again, the group may wish to express that excuse in words that Jesus could have used.

C. Help group members analyze what was in fact Jesus' response. Have the group discuss each of these points:

 1. Jesus knew what a realistic inventory of needs and resources would reveal. (Read the words of Philip and Andrew.)

 2. Nevertheless, Jesus took responsibility. He had the people sit down.

 3. Jesus gave thanks for what he had.

 4. Through God's power, Jesus was able to feed the multitude.

D. Invite the group to reflect on one of the urgent needs that they see around them in their community, in the country, or in the larger world. Preferably, to keep the subject more connected with the session theme, it should be a need for food—hunger in another country, in your city, among the homeless, among older adults, and so forth. But it could be another material need. Once you have identified the need to be discussed, go back to the chalkboard or large sheet of paper and add an additional line to each of the three columns you had there, as follows:

Friend A	Friend B	Friend C
the needy	disciple	God
the multitude	Jesus	God
(whatever the need)	us	God

E. Go back to the list of possible excuses (**B.1–3**) and ask the group to state each of those excuses with reference to the need you are discussing: the "spiritual excuse," the "purity excuse," and the "pragmatic excuse." In line with what we have been studying, ask them also to respond to each of those excuses.

F. Look at the analysis of Jesus' response in **C.1–4**; then ask the group to perform the same analysis with reference to the need you have decided to discuss. Raise the following issues:

1. Ask: *What would a realistic inventory of our resources show?* Encourage the group to think not only of their own personal financial resources but also of their influence on others, their political power, their various fields of expertise, and so forth. List these resources on the chalkboard or large sheet of paper.

2. Ask: *Jesus took responsibility by inviting the crowd to sit down. How can we show that we actually take responsibility for the need we are discussing?*

3. Jesus gave thanks over the meager amount of food available. Explain that giving thanks is crucial in this process because by doing so we acknowledge that all these things that we have listed in our inventory actually come from God. They are not strictly ours, even though they might include our education or our bank account. To give thanks, therefore, means to put it all at God's disposal. Ask group members to give thoughtful consideration to this question: *Are we ready to do that?*

4. Finally, note that Jesus used what he had and left the rest in God's hands. Ask: *What would it mean for us to use what we have listed in our inventory? How would we begin doing that? What would be the next steps? How can we support one another as we take those steps?*

G. Bring the class to a close by praying for the guidance of the Holy Spirit as you and the other members of the group seek to make use of your inventory of resources for meeting the needs you encounter.

Chapter 4: Healing [pages 43–52]

Preparation. Today's session gives opportunity for bringing the biblical passage to life. You may want group members to "get into character" before your time together, although this is not necessary. If you do want them to prepare in advance, tell members which character they will be taking and ask them to reflect on that person's or group's role in the story.

If you plan to have someone speak to the class about your church's or denomination's work in the area of healing ministry as suggested in **I**, contact that person several days before class. Also, gather information on this issue from denominational agencies ahead of time; and find out about your own church's involvement.

Have a chalkboard and chalk or a large sheet of paper and a marker available.

A. Open the session with prayer, asking God to help your group bring today's passage from Mark to life.

B. Create a cast of characters and set the scene for the biblical story:
1. Ask someone to be Bartimaeus. Put a blanket on that person's seat so that Bartimaeus can be sitting, half wrapped in his cloak. Tell this person that Bartimaeus comes from a very poor family, is unable to see, and ekes out an existence by begging.
2. Choose some other group members (the number will depend on the size of your group) to be disciples. Tell them they have been following Jesus for some time, hoping that he will prove to be the Messiah, the Son of David who will restore the kingdom of Israel.
3. Ask two or three others to act as informers. Tell them their sympathies are with the existing religious and political leaders, and they are mingling with the crowd to see what Jesus is about—in order to go tell the authorities.
4. Finally, have the rest of the group be the crowd. Tell them they are curious, following to see what happens, some perhaps hoping that Jesus will turn out to be the Messiah and others hoping that he will get in trouble so they can see a good show.

C. Ask the characters to use their imagination to get into the role assigned to them, and have each of them (or each group) describe for the larger group who they are and what they think.
1. Bartimaeus is to explain his name, what he is doing sitting by the roadside, and something about his cloak.
2. The disciples are to express their hopes and fears, now that Jesus is finally on the last leg of the journey to Jerusalem.

19

3. The informers can tell what they intend to do if they find out that Jesus is really a subversive with plans to overthrow the government and claim the throne of David.
4. The curious hangers-on can say something about what they are looking for.

D. Before you move on, read aloud 2 Samuel 5:6-8. Explain to the group that most of the crowd, being Jews, would know that story and therefore would not expect anyone like David to have concern for the blind. Certainly, David did not let the blind stop him.

E. Now have "Bartimaeus" shout the words in verse 47. Point out that this is the first time in the Gospel of Mark that Jesus is called "Son of David." Then ask the "disciples" how they feel. (Most likely, knowing that there may be informers around, they want the beggar to be quiet.) Ask the same thing of the "informers" and of the "hangers-on." Make certain that someone points out the possible connection between this story and the one in Second Samuel. Have the beggar shout again, this time using the words in verse 48.

F. Read the rest of today's Scripture passage and ask each character or each group to describe their reaction to the story.

G. You may wish to have the class comment on some other points raised in *When Christ Lives in Us*:
1. Invite group members to comment on the contrast between the "seeing" disciples who are blind in Mark 10:35-45 and this blind man who sees in Mark 10:46-52.
2. Ask: *Why would many among those with Jesus sharply order Bartimaeus to be quiet?*
3. Jesus stopped. Ask: *Is there any connection between Jesus stopping as recorded in this passage and his having the hungry crowd sit down as recorded in John 6 (see Chapter 3, above)?* (Both are signs that Jesus takes responsibility, in one case for the hungry and in the other for the blind.)
4. Ask: *What is the significance of Jesus asking Bartimaeus what he wanted?* (Healing in the Spirit of Christ involves a restoration of dignity.)
5. Jesus did not require that the man follow him in order to

receive healing. Indeed, Jesus told him to "go"; for he could see! Ask: *What is the significance of Jesus telling the now well man to "go"?* (Jesus did not set conditions on helping people.)

H. The book says that in the context of disease and healing, there are three courses of action that should not be open to us as Christians [pages 51–52]. List each of these on a chalkboard or on a large sheet of paper; then ask members of the group if they have ever heard such opinions expressed by well-intentioned Christians. If possible, have group members give concrete examples. Then read the statements aloud, asking after each: *What do you think is wrong with this statement?*

I. Now turn to your own church's ministry of healing. Before the class convenes, investigate what your church is doing in this area. Perhaps it is acting directly; or perhaps it is contributing to the world mission of the church at large, which in turn includes much work of healing. If there is someone in your congregation with special knowledge about this, invite that person to explain briefly what the church is doing by way of healing. Or gather materials from The United Methodist Committee on Relief (UMCOR) or your denominational agency in charge of these matters, distribute those materials, and discuss them briefly. The group will probably discover that there is much that the church is doing of which they ought to be proud.

J. Widen the discussion by explaining that "healing" does not necessarily have to be medical. We can also heal broken relationships and broken lives. Give some examples.

K. Ask some concrete questions to invite the members of your group to participate in this ministry: *Who in our community is calling for us to stop, like Bartimaeus, a blind man? What are some of the more glaring hurts and diseases in our community? What would be for us the equivalent of stopping, listening, and trying to heal?* List responses on the chalkboard or on the large sheet of paper.

L. At this point in the session, you may refer the group again to the parable of the three friends [pages 27–29]. Ask: *In each of the needs that we have listed together, what can we do as Friend B? What resources do we actually have to respond to the need? Having committed those resources, what other resources should we ask from Friend C (God)?* Again, list responses on the chalkboard or on the large sheet of paper.

M. Close the session with a prayer mentioning the needs listed, committing the resources listed to the needy and to God, and asking God for those resources that are lacking.

Chapter 5: Commissioning [pages 53–64]

Preparation. Have a chalkboard and chalk or a large sheet of paper and a marker available. If this is to be your last session together, plan ahead on how you will close the session. Also consider ways by which the group members can continue to support one another in living out your calls and commissions.

A. Open the session with prayer; then have someone read aloud today's passage of Scripture. Encourage the group to focus for a moment on those who doubted. Summarize (or have someone else summarize) what the book says about doubt and disobedience [pages 54–55]. Then lead the class in exploring some issues related to doubt and despair.

1. Tell the group that a Christian Guatemalan poet, Julia Esquivel, has written a book entitled *Threatened With Resurrection* (Brethren Press, 1994). Her point there is that the Resurrection, in a sense, makes things more difficult. Now there is hope; and because there is hope, one must continue to struggle. Without the Resurrection, she and the other Guatemalan Christians who have lost so much could simply give in to despair. That would make life much simpler. But the Resurrection rules out that possibility and is therefore a threat.

2. Invite the group to close their eyes and imagine that they are the disciples. After three years of wandering and hoping, their dreams are now shattered. Deeply disappointed, they are getting ready to return home to their old lives and their old routines. It is seemingly time to pick up the pieces and move on. Ask: *In such circumstances, would you be inclined to doubt or to have faith? Why?*

3. After members have had a chance to respond, ask: *In what ways are we "threatened with Resurrection"? When do we doubt because to believe would launch us into risky and costly adventures?* Invite the group to give examples if they wish.

B. Jesus commissioned those who doubted as well as those who worshiped him. The book suggests that being sent to make disciples may well be the best medicine for doubting disciples [page 57]. Ask: *Do you agree? Why or why not?* Invite group members to tell of experiences similar to what the book describes, of the author coming to greater faith by the very act of communicating the faith.

C. Now pose the opposite question: *Could it be that one reason our faith is not as deep as it should be is that we do not share it as we should?* Encourage group members to comment on this question.

D. The book says that all Christians are commissioned [page 59]. If that is true, it means that in some sense Jesus has a commission for each of the members of your group. Can the group as a whole help its individual members discover what their calling and commission may be? Plan to spend at least an hour on this point.
   1. Begin with a time of prayer, asking for guidance in what the group is about to discuss.
   2. Ask members of the group to share the following:
      a. Feelings or thoughts they may have had that they are called to a particular form of Christian service.
      b. Feelings or thoughts they may have that one of the other members of the group may be called to a particular form of Christian service.
   3. After meeting for five extensive sessions, as you have, group members should feel comfortable enough to help one another explore these possibilities. Therefore, discuss as openly as possible what various members have said about their possible calling or the calling of others. You may want to list these callings on a chalkboard or on a large sheet of paper.
   4. This discussion should include the difficulties or negative factors that people see in such callings. (For instance, someone may say, "I feel called to ordained ministry, but I am afraid of

having to go back to school." Or, "Mary is apparently called to visit the sick; but she is afraid that when she gets there, she will not know what to say or do.") As with the callings, list these difficulties on the chalkboard or large sheet of paper.

E. To deal with such potential difficulties, go back to the beginning of the chapter in the book [pages 53–54], to the meaning of the phrase "All authority in heaven and on earth has been given to me." By means of a few questions and/or a short explanation, help members of the group understand the far-reaching import of this assertion. It does *not* mean that everything will be easy. It *does* mean that, no matter where you are going, Jesus is already there even before you set out on the journey.

F. Return to the difficulties or obstacles that people have listed and invite group members to make a covenant that you will help one another in taking whatever steps are necessary to fulfill your callings. (*Ask permission* from the group to report about this to the pastor and other people who may be of assistance. Perhaps the group and the pastor will agree that some of these people should be formally commissioned and recognized by the congregation for whatever their calling is.)

G. If this is the last session in which the group will be meeting (a VBS group, for example), you may wish to do a number of things before closing the session (If this is not the last session, skip **G** and go on to **H.**):
1. Have the group decide what to do about the three chapters in the book you have not studied. Group members may elect to read them in private; to schedule three more sessions, perhaps in consecutive weeks; or to meet in twos or threes for informal conversations about the material. Whatever group members decide, it is important that all of you have a sense that the group has not simply disappeared. There is a continuing link, perhaps in further study of the remaining chapters, but certainly in prayer.
2. Connect what you have said here regarding commissioning with what was said in the first chapter regarding calling. Remember: Jesus called Simon and the others not only to

follow him but also to become something they were not: fishers of people. Likewise, our calling implies also a sending, a new reality that we are to become. In some ways that is the goal of discipleship, and for that reason it makes sense to end our study at this point.

3. Make it clear that being sent also involves searching for others who are to be sent in turn—in other words, that we are *called to call* and *commissioned to commission*. Thus, whatever we have decided to undertake as the next step in our discipleship is not really the end of something but part of a long chain, generations long, of commissioned commissioners. It is that chain that we are now joining.

4. Close the session with a prayer of thanksgiving for the gospel, for one another, for this study, and for the new future that now opens before us.

H. If this is not the last session of your study, point out that this lesson is a turning point; for here we have come full circle to the full meaning of calling, which was the subject of the first lesson. (See above, **G.2.**) The next three lessons will deal with specific things for which we—all of us—are commissioned: teaching, witnessing, and giving. Close the session with prayer.

Chapter 6: Teaching [pages 65–73]

Preparation. Have a chalkboard and chalk or a large sheet of paper and a marker available. Have enough NRSV Bibles on hand for each group member to read along.

A. Open the session with prayer, inviting the Holy Spirit to teach you all as you study today's passage from Matthew together.

B. Introduce the study with a general discussion of teaching and its authority. In that discussion, stress the following:

1. Our Scripture passage raises a profound question: What gives someone authority to teach? Ask: **What qualifications do you expect a teacher to have?** (Things such as "knowledge of the subject matter," "know how to teach," "respect for students,"

25

and so forth could be mentioned.) List the group's responses on a chalkboard or on a large sheet of paper.

2. In a traditional culture the main function of a teacher is to pass on the tradition. The society entrusts its upcoming generations to teachers who will socialize them into the mores and customs of the group as a whole. In such a society teachers, as depositories of the values and traditions of the community, are highly respected and are seldom controversial. (You may point out that, to a large extent, that was the case in our society in the early 1900's.)

3. This function is disrupted when a teacher (or teachers) disagrees with some aspect of the tradition. At that point, there is a clash of authorities: that of the tradition versus whatever claim the teacher has for his or her own doctrines. (Mention the Scopes trial of 1925, when a young teacher taught evolution and the community resented it.) Then the question is, Whose authority will prevail?

4. To some degree, this clash is what is going on in Jesus' teachings. As a rabbi he is supposed to uphold the tradition—and he does. But he interprets the tradition differently than do those who are officially in charge of that interpretation. The clash is inevitable.

C. Now look at some of the teachings of Jesus in light of that clash of authorities. Take about an hour to study Luke 15:

1. Invite the group to take on the roles of Pharisees and scribes. Explain what these words meant (you may look them up in *The Interpreter's Dictionary of the Bible* [Abingdon, 1962] or another Bible dictionary). Emphasize the point that these were good, faithful, religious people. As far as religion goes, they were very much the "in" group. Ask: ***Who would be the scribes and Pharisees today?***

2. Once the group members are into their roles, read aloud Luke 15:1; then ask them to react to it. Compare their reaction with what is described in Luke 15:2. If their reaction is quite different, insist that they must get into their roles!

3. Now read aloud Luke 15:3-10, emphasizing the word "them" in verse 3. (In other words, these parables are addressed to the Pharisees and scribes.)

4. Ask the "Pharisees and scribes" how they react.

5. Repeat the process with Luke 15:11-32, still making the point that Jesus is speaking to the Pharisees and scribes.

6. Encourage the group to read some of the other parables when they are back at home, taking into account to whom Jesus is speaking (for instance, the rich man and Lazarus [Luke 16:14-31] or the Pharisee and the tax collector [Luke 18:9-14]).

D. Ask: *Why did Jesus speak in parables?* Encourage group members to give their opinions. Make sure the group is aware of the following three reasons, the first two of which are often overlooked:

1. Some of the things Jesus said would have caused him grave and immediate trouble if he had said them plainly. Remember that at his trial he was accused of having said something he did not say about destroying and rebuilding the Temple. His enemies were waiting around, hanging on every word, to catch him in a seditious or subversive or blasphemous saying. Instead, he spoke in parables and let his hearers decide on their meaning.

2. A parable neither condemns nor justifies. It forces one to place oneself in the story. Thus it can be quite harsh and still leave the way open for grace.

3. For the same reason, a parable gives little information but can be very valuable in shaping one's life. If you put yourself at a certain place in the story (for instance, the parable of the lost coin or the lost sheep or the lost son), your entire life may change.

E. Return to the question of authority. Ask: *By what authority did Jesus teach?* (Here you may summarize what the book says about "authority" and "authorship" [pages 66–68].)

F. Focus the attention of the group on the scope of Jesus' teachings. Ask: *What did Jesus teach about?* List the answers (things like "sheep," "fish," "baking," "plowing," "family," "money," and so forth) on the chalkboard or the large sheet of paper. Relate this to the question of authority raised in section E above and to what we saw in Chapter 5: All things are under Jesus' authority—and come from his authorship. There is nothing that is not capable of being used for teaching because all things are under his authority.

G. As a final subject for discussion, ask: *How is our teaching similar to Jesus'? How is it different? As people called to teach, what can we learn from Jesus as a teacher?*

H. Close the session with prayer, inviting people to call out what they have learned from Jesus as a teacher and then having the group respond, "For this we give thanks, O God." End the prayer with an expression of thanks for the opportunity to teach others.

Chapter 7: Witnessing [pages 74–84]

Preparation. Have a chalkboard and chalk or a large sheet of paper and a marker available. For **B**, several days before the session ask someone to consult a concordance and count all the references in Matthew, Mark, and Luke to the *kingdom of God* and to the *kingdom of heaven*. For **E**, before the session look up the word *witness* in a dictionary or two and write out the definitions relating to seeing and telling on two separate sheets of paper.

A. Open the session with prayer; then have someone read aloud the passage of Scripture (Acts 1:6-8). Give the group a few moments to reflect on the passage.

B. Begin by asking: *What it is that the disciples expect when they ask if Jesus is about to "restore the kingdom to Israel"?* Point out that Jesus corrects them and that it is important to see where they were wrong and where they were right:

1. The disciples *were right* in asking about the Kingdom. Several days before the session, ask one of the group to consult a concordance and count all the references in Matthew, Mark, and Luke to the *kingdom of God* and to the *kingdom of heaven*. Have that person report to the group at this point in the session. It will be obvious that the "kingdom of God" is very important in both Mark and Luke and that Matthew prefers the phrase "kingdom of heaven." Explain that the two mean exactly the same thing, for Matthew is simply using the Jewish custom at the time of speaking of "heaven" instead of

referring directly to God. Underscore the point that according to the Gospels the kingdom or reign of God is central to Jesus' message.

2. The disciples *were wrong* in asking about the time. Read Jesus' response to their question and lead the group in a discussion clarifying this point.

3. The disciples *were also wrong* in limiting the Kingdom to Israel. Again, read Jesus' response and lead a discussion clarifying the point.

4. *Perhaps* (the text does not say so) the disciples were wrong in thinking that the Kingdom would come with the same sort of power as common, everyday, earthly kingdoms. Invite group members to comment on this issue.

C. Having considered what was wrong with the disciples' question, have the group reflect on contemporary examples of those errors. Ask: *Do we ever make any of those errors? If so, in what ways?* As members respond, you may wish to help them think about the following, each of which relates to one of the disciples' errors:

1. Recently, there has been a spate of books and constant predictions about the end—how and when it will come.

2. Christians of a particular denomination or ethnic tradition sometimes have difficulty accepting others as Christians.

3. Many church members across the political spectrum hold to the notion that, if the church only had more political influence or more money or better organization, we could do more to bring about the Kingdom. Of course, these things may be good if used wisely; but if the church tries to wield "power" just as the world does, then it is as salt that has lost its flavor.

D. Now move more specifically to the matter of witnessing. Divide a chalkboard or large sheet of paper into three columns with three headings: "Teacher," "Both," and "Witness." Ask the group to list some things that distinguish a teacher from a witness, some things that distinguish a witness from a teacher, and some things that are common to both. (The book [pages 78–80] may be helpful at this point, but do encourage the group to think on their own about teachers and witnesses they have known or seen.)

E. Before the session, look up the word *witness* in a dictionary or two. You will note that some definitions refer to seeing or being present when an event takes place, while others refer to speaking about it—often in a court of law. Write both of these definitions on a separate large sheet of paper. At this point in the session, put up the two sheets; have the group discuss the definitions; and then write on a chalkboard or on another large piece of paper in big letters "seeing" and "telling."

    1. Ask: *How is it that a witness to Christ sees Christ?* (Obviously, it is by the power of the Holy Spirit that we become, so to speak, contemporaries of Jesus so that we come to know him and believe in him. It is that experience that constitutes the basis of Christian witness.)

    2. Ask: *How is it that a witness to Christ tells about Christ?* At this point, encourage the group to be very specific: How and where is it that we witness or can witness to Christ? Invite members to share stories of success as well as confessions of fear and of failure.

F. Remind the group of what we saw in Chapter 5, that Jesus commissioned even those who had been doubting and that this commissioning may be a good remedy for doubt. Ask: *Do you think that if we were more active in our witness, our faith would be strengthened? Or do you think that we have to wait until we have more faith before we shall be able to witness more effectively?* Encourage members of the group to give examples, from their own experience or from that of others, of how witnessing strengthens faith. Invite them to go on record that they are willing to "give it a try" and to make it a point to witness to their faith in Christ and see what happens to that faith. (If you receive positive responses to the invitation, you may wish to follow up with some concrete plans, not only for action but also for support of those who are witnessing.)

G. Close the session with a prayer in which the group asks for the power of the Spirit in order to witness wherever they may be.

Chapter 8: Giving [pages 85–95]

Preparation. Have a chalkboard and chalk or a large sheet of paper and a marker available. Prepare "G.F.P. Worksheets" as outlined in **H**, enough for each member of the group to have one.

A. Open the session with prayer, thanking God for the time the group has spent together and asking for the guidance of the Holy Spirit as you explore the meaning of giving.

B. The book claims that all that has been studied in the previous chapters can be summarized in the word *giving* [page 85]. Ask group members to comment on this statement. Do they believe it is true? Invite them to look at the Contents page of *When Christ Lives in Us* and to reflect on how giving is involved in each of the subjects treated:

1. **Chapter 1.** Ask: *What did Jesus give to those whom he called?* (He gave them a new name, a new mission, a new reality.)
2. **Chapter 2.** Ask: *How did Jesus relate prayer to giving and to receiving?* (Think of the parable of the three friends, the prayer for daily bread, receiving the gift of the Spirit, and so forth.)
3. **Chapter 3.** Ask: *What did Jesus do before giving food to the multitude?* (He made an inventory of available resources and gave thanks to God for them.)
4. **Chapter 4.** Ask: *What did Jesus give to Bartimaeus?* (He gave the man a sense of dignity, and he gave him physical well-being.)
5. **Chapter 5.** Ask: *How is the act of commissioning a gift?* (Jesus gives his followers, both those of strong faith and those who have doubts, the opportunity to mature in faith and practice in becoming part of a long chain of those sent to proclaim the gospel.)
6. **Chapter 6.** Ask: *What did Jesus give as teacher?* (He gave insight into the kingdom of God, insight that could help change a person's life.)
7. **Chapter 7.** Ask: *What does a witness give?* (A witness tells what he or she has seen—tells his or her story—in the hope that it will benefit others.)

C. The book talks about how a gift can be unwelcome [pages 86–88]. Ask the group to tell stories about unwelcome gifts in their experience. As they share such stories, write on a chalkboard or on a large sheet of paper a word or two suggesting a reason why a gift might not be welcome. (For instance, if someone tells of a person fighting alcoholism being given a case of champagne, write "callous." If someone tells of a man with a beard receiving shaving cream, write "useless." If someone tells of a gift so valuable that it requires a similar gift in return, write "burdensome." Other possible words would be "humiliating," "grudging," "ostentatious," and "miserly.")

D. Ask: *When we say that the gift of Christ is sometimes unwelcome, what are our reasons? Look at the words on the chalkboard (or sheet of paper). Do any of them apply? Why or why not? Are there other reasons? What is required of those who accept the gift of Christ?*

E. Much of the chapter in the book deals with gift giving at Christmas and claims that quite often all the noise and activity at Yuletide becomes a way to avoid receiving the Gift that Christmas is all about. Ask: *Do you agree? Why or why not?* Some more specific questions are:
1. *Have you found some of your Christmas shopping and giving actually a chore? If so, why? What is missing?*
2. *When have you found yourself trying to buy presents for someone who "has it all" and racking your brain because you feel obligated to give that person something?*
3. *Why is the Christmas season busier than it should be—busy with activities that have little to do with the birth of Jesus?*

   (If group members wish to pursue the matter this coming Christmas, you may encourage them to send for the booklet "Whose Birthday Is It, Anyway?" from Alternatives, Inc., P.O. Box 2857, Sioux City, Iowa 51106. Phone: (712)-274-8875.

F. The book suggests that giving involves more than money. Ask the group to name nonmonetary gifts we can give, listing each on a chalkboard or large sheet of paper. (Some examples include time; words or gestures of support; and knowledge, expertise, or abilities.) For each gift listed, ask: *What makes this gift valuable?*

G. Now turn the question around and ask the group to suggest ways in which we misuse, cheapen, waste, or exploit each of the gifts you have listed.

H. The book suggests a similarity between physical fitness and giving [pages 93–94]. Both require exercise and discipline. Suggest that just as some of us have—and all of us should have—a physical fitness program, perhaps we should also have a "Giving Fitness Program"—a "G.F.P." for short. After discussing this matter briefly, give each person a "G.F.P. Worksheet," as outlined below. Ask the group members to spend some time in quiet reflection and prayer and then to outline for themselves—that is, for their own private use—what would be a good personal program of "giving fitness." Explain that no one else is to see this document; they will keep it for future reference as a gauge of their progress in their G.F.P.

The G.F.P. Worksheet should say:

I have 24 hours a day and 7 days a week; a measure of my G.F.P. in the use of time will be that _____.

I have the following gifts and expertise. A measure of my G.F.P. in their use will be that _____.

I make $_____ a (week) (month) (year). A measure of my G.F.P. in the use of money will be that _____.

I. As a final meditation, before the closing prayer you may wish to read aloud the "Unconclusion" of the book [page 96], explaining beforehand that, although this is a farewell from the author, it may also be read as a farewell from the members of the group to one another.

J. Close the session with a prayer in which you give thanks for the study, dedicate the programs for "giving fitness" that people have set up for themselves, and ask for God's guidance as each person continues in her or his spiritual pilgrimage.

Part II

Use in Sunday School Classes (Eight Sessions)

The book *When Christ Lives in Us* may be used as a resource for a Sunday school class. As compared with the settings discussed in **Part I** of this Leader's Guide, such a setting has both advantages and disadvantages. The major disadvantage is that the study group will have less than an hour to spend on each chapter—unless the group decides to study the book at a rate of less than a chapter a week. Another disadvantage is that in Sunday school classes attendance is less likely to be constant. There will be visitors who will attend only a single session of your study or members who for whatever reason miss one or more sessions. So each session must have its own coherence and integrity even for those who do not follow the entire study.

The major advantage of studying the book as part of a Sunday school program is that Sunday school classes have greater permanence. Therefore the group members will feel more comfortable with one another, with the possibility of more openness in discussing matters as intimate as one's relationship with God, one's sense of calling, and one's obedience or disobedience to such calling. Also, the members of a Sunday school class may decide on long-term commitments to one another or to some specific project in the community as a result of taking part in this study.

In the sections that follow, it is taken for granted that the Sunday school class will devote one session of forty to fifty minutes to each chapter of the book. If that is not the case and you have more than that amount of time available, look back in **Part I** of this Leader's Guide, where you will find additional materials, questions for discussion, and learning activities.

Again, as in the case of the use of the book in small groups or in vacation Bible school, this Leader's Guide takes for granted that Sunday school class participants will have read each chapter of the book before the class meets to study and discuss it. (See the reasons for doing so in **Part I, Use in Small Groups and Vacation Bible School**, page 6.)

****

34

The leader's material for the Sunday school class study of *When Christ Lives in Us* is organized by the chapters of the book. Note that all page numbers in brackets refer to *When Christ Lives in Us*—for example, [pages 10–20]—while other page numbers refer to this Leader's Guide.

Within the chapter divisions, successive themes are indicated by bold capital letters (**A.**, **B.**, **C.**) and successive questions or activities around these themes by bold Arabic numerals (**1.**, **2.**, **3.**). Options in method are indicated by **OR**. Of course, leaders may choose among themes, questions, and activities to customize the session for their class and time frame.

Chapter 1: Calling [pages 10–20]

Preparation. Have a chalkboard and chalk or a large sheet of paper and a marker available. For **D.2**, think of some names that would be appropriate for the exercise. For **E**, have nametags available for each class member.

A. Lead the class in prayer; then introduce the subject of our study. Ask the class members to open their Bibles and follow along while someone reads aloud Matthew 4:18-22.

B. Lead the class in a discussion of this passage of Scripture. Make certain that in the discussion at least the following points are highlighted:
1. When Jesus called these four men, he called them not just to follow him but also to become something they were not. (From fishers of fish, they were to become fishers of people.)
2. This new reality Jesus called into being is symbolized in Simon's change of name. He was *Simon*, but later Jesus called him *Peter (Rock)* and made him what he called him, a rock.
3. When Jesus called them, these four not only had to become something new; they also had to leave behind some of the things connected with their prior lives—their nets, their boat, their father.

C. Help the class understand the significance of what we are called—including our name—by using any of the methods suggested in **Part I, Chapter I, C** (pages 8–10).

35

D. Now help the class members think about their calling by using the following procedure:

1. Remind them that in the monastic tradition many people change their names when they become monks or nuns. By that change of name they symbolize what they hope to be, by God's grace and calling. For instance, a woman whose name is Jane may take the monastic name Sister Charity, indicating that she feels called to a life of love and that she hopes love will be a central characteristic of her life and personality as they develop in the convent. Or a man called Richard may take the monastic name Basil or Francis because Saint Basil or Saint Francis is the model after whom he hopes to shape his life. Remind the participants also that at times people being baptized as adults have chosen to change their names as a sign of the radical change, the new birth, that their baptism indicated.

2. Now ask members of the class to reflect on what would be appropriate names for them—names indicating what they are called to be or who they are. Do this by dividing the class into pairs or into groups of three and having each group discuss what are some of the gifts and positive traits of each of its members, what they feel that particular person is called to be or to do, or what are some of the gifts that person has. On that basis, ask each small group to "name" each of its members. (In other words, people are not to name themselves but rather to allow the other or others to name them.) In order to facilitate this exercise, suggest some names. Some of these could be names that have a meaning in themselves, such as Hope or Faith. Others could be names that derive their meaning from people who have had them in the past. For example, someone who is always seeking to reform things could be called Martin Luther; a good musician could be John Sebastian (after Bach); a good care giver could be Martha; a letter writer could be Paul. And some may even be made-up names for this particular person, such as Helper, Doer, Treasurer, Teach, Thinker, Letsgettogether, or Doitright. Include yourself in the process so that you too will have a name suggested by the class.

E. You may wish to continue discussion of this subject later in this study as suggested in this Leader's Guide (since in some future sessions nametags are used, you may wish to glance quickly at the rest of the Leader's Guide before deciding whether to include this step in this session). If so, give class members blank nametags and ask them to write on them their own name as well as the "name" that they have been given if they believe it is accurate. If they do not feel that name is appropriate, they may write another name that they prefer. After the session collect the nametags; distribute them each Sunday at the beginning of the session for the class members to wear as a way to help them recollect earlier sessions and also as an invitation for each of them to think about his or her own calling. Again, include yourself in this process, making your own nametag. (If others join the class in later sessions, you may wish to invite them to a special discussion in which you review this first lesson so they too will have nametags and not be left out whenever such tags are part of the session.)

F. Finally, point out that our various callings to discipleship, no matter how varied, all call us to call others. We are called so that we too may go and call. (See **Part I, Chapter I, F**, pages 11–12.)

G. Close the session with a prayer, thanking God for the call to discipleship extended to each class member and asking for courage, power, and wisdom to call others.

Chapter 2: Praying [pages 21–31]

Preparation. Distribute the nametags you have made in the previous session, explain briefly the meaning of the tags, and ask those who have not been given tags if they wish to have one. Collect the nametags at the close of class.

For **C**, you may want to talk with people a few days before class about taking part in the roleplay. If you wish to relate the parable of the friends to our life of prayer and response to need as in **E**, bring several recent newspapers to class.

Have a chalkboard and chalk or a large sheet of paper and a marker available.

A. Open the class with prayer; then offer a brief review of last week's class. Stress the point that the life of discipleship is a life of calling and that, although each one of us has a different calling, we are all called to call others to discipleship.

B. Emphasize the plural "we" in the Lord's Prayer. You may do this by one of the two procedures outlined in **Part I, Chapter 2, C** (page 13). Suggest that the next time they pray the Lord's Prayer, class members think about different possible meanings of the word *we*:

1. Ask: *How does* **we** *refer to those of us gathered, praying together?*
2. Ask: *How does* **we** *refer to all of our congregation, no matter where they may be?*
3. Ask: *How does* **we** *refer to all Christians throughout the world?*
4. Ask: *How does* **we** *refer to all of creation, calling on the Creator?*

C. Move to the parable that follows the Lord's Prayer in Luke. Discuss its meaning following the alternatives suggested under **Part I, Chapter 2, F** (page 14). One possible way to do this would be by means of roleplaying. Ask someone with a creative and dramatic flair to be "Friend B." Ask two other people to be "Friend A" and "Friend C." Have them act out each of the four scenarios described in **Part I, Chapter 2, F.** (At the beginning of each short skit, you may describe the situation and ask the actors to improvise. Or, you may give them beforehand a copy of the four scenarios and ask them to prepare very short skits of no more than two minutes apiece for each of those situations.)

D. After the skits, present the class with a "Friend A" who is coming to us for help. (This person may symbolize famine in some part of the world, the homeless in your own town, or someone who is bereaved. Choose what seems best for your class.) Ask the members to discuss what the four skits and the parable that they illumine mean for our Christian responsibility, and then invite them to comment on the place of prayer in our response to such needs.

E. You may wish to guide a discussion as outlined in **Part I, Chapter 2, G** (pages 14–15).

OR

F. You may wish to have class members reflect on what resources they have for those in need in light of the new names (recorded on the nametags) that members were given in the last session.

G. Close the session with prayer, thanking God for the opportunities and obligations of prayer.

Chapter 3: Feeding [pages 32–42]

Preparation. Distribute the nametags you have made in a previous session, explain briefly the meaning of the tags, and ask those who have not been given tags if they wish to have one. Collect the nametags at the close of class.

You will need to have a chalkboard and chalk or a large sheet of paper and a marker available.

A. Invite someone to open class with a prayer. Then read aloud the Scripture passage for this session.

B. Quickly review last week's parable and show its connection with today's passage. As you speak, write on a chalkboard or on a large piece of paper the three columns below, which display the relationship between the passages:

Friend A	Friend B	Friend C
the needy	disciple	God
the multitude	Jesus	God

C. The book points out that Jesus could have pled two excuses: the "spiritual excuse" [pages 33–35] and the "purity excuse" [pages 35–36]. Review these two excuses with the class, explaining each as briefly as possible.

D. Invite the class to reflect on one of the urgent needs related to hunger that they see around them in their community, in the country, or in the larger world. Once you have identified the need to be discussed, go back to the chalkboard or large sheet of paper and add an additional line to each of the three columns you had there:

Friend A	Friend B	Friend C
the needy	disciple	God
the multitude	Jesus	God
(whatever the need)	us	God

E. Return to the two possible excuses (**C**, above) and ask the class to state each of those excuses with reference to the need you have identified. Then ask them also to critique each of those excuses.

F. Relate Jesus' response to need as shown in today's biblical passage to our response. Raise the following issues:

1. Ask: *Jesus made a realistic inventory of available resources. What would a realistic inventory of our resources show?* Encourage the group to think not only of their own personal financial resources but also of their influence on others, their political power, their various fields of expertise, and so forth. List these resources on the chalkboard or large sheet of paper.
2. Ask: *Jesus took responsibility by inviting the crowd to sit down. How can we show that we actually take responsibility for the need we are discussing?*
3. Jesus gave thanks over the meager amount of food available. Explain that giving thanks is crucial in this process because by doing so we acknowledge that all the things we have listed in our inventory actually come from God. To give thanks, therefore, means to put our all at God's disposal. Ask group members to give thoughtful consideration to this question: *Are we ready to put our all at God's disposal?*
4. Finally, note that Jesus used what he had and left the rest in God's hands. Ask: *What would it mean for us to use what we have listed in our inventory? How would we begin doing that? What would be the next steps? How can we support one another as we take those steps?*

G. Ask the class members to mention things for which they would like to give thanks. These may include some of the things listed in their inventory of resources and/or others. The important point is that by giving thanks over something, we are placing whatever it is at God's disposal. Then lead the class (or ask someone else to lead) in a prayer giving thanks for the things mentioned and listed and asking God to use them to help meet the needs of the world.

****

Chapter 4: Healing [pages 43–52]

Preparation. Distribute the nametags you have made in a previous session, explain briefly the meaning of the tags, and ask those who have not been given tags if they wish to have one. Collect the nametags at the close of class.

Today's session gives opportunity for bringing the biblical passage to life. You may want class members to "get into character" before your time together, although this is not necessary. If you do want them to prepare in advance, tell members which character they will be taking and ask them to reflect on that person's or group's role in the story.

For E, write out the three statements, one on each of three large pieces of paper. For F, inquire about a healing ministry in which your church is involved. If the ministry is nearby, plan a visit with two or three class members. If it is farther away, collect some relevant information and give it to one of the class members (or ask him or her to collect it). Thus, someone will be ready with a brief report.

A. Open the session with prayer, asking God to help your class bring today's passage from Mark to life.

B. Create a cast of characters and set the scene for the biblical story:
1. Ask someone to be Bartimaeus. Put a blanket on that person's seat so that Bartimaeus can be sitting, half wrapped in his cloak. Tell this person that Bartimaeus comes from a very poor family, is unable to see, and ekes out an existence by begging.
2. Choose some other class members (the number will depend on the size of your class) to be disciples. Tell them they have been following Jesus for some time, hoping that he will prove to be the Messiah, the Son of David who will restore the kingdom of Israel.
3. Ask two or three others to act as informers. Tell them their sympathies are with the existing religious and political leaders, and they are mingling with the crowd to see what Jesus is about—in order to go tell the authorities.
4. Finally, have the rest of the class be the crowd. Tell them they are curious, following to see what happens, some perhaps hoping that Jesus will turn out to be the Messiah and others hoping that he will get in trouble so they can see a good show.

41

C. Before having class members bring the text to life, read aloud 2 Samuel 5:6-8. Explain that most of the crowd, being Jews, would know that story and therefore would not expect anyone like David to have concern for the blind. Certainly, David did not let the blind stop him.

D. Now have "Bartimaeus" shout the words in verse 47. Point out that this is the first time in the Gospel of Mark that Jesus is called "Son of David." Then ask the "disciples" how they feel. (Most likely, knowing that there may be informers around, they want the beggar to be quiet.) Ask the same thing of the "informers" and of the "hangers-on." Make certain that someone points out the possible connection between this story and the one in Second Samuel. Have the beggar shout again, this time using the words in verse 48. Then read the rest of today's Scripture passage and ask each character or each group to describe their reaction to the story.

E. Have the class consider the following three statements, which you have written out on three pieces of paper in advance:

(1) "When Christians heal someone or help someone in any way, they should not mention the name of Jesus or say anything that may sound like witnessing to Jesus or trying to bring people to faith in him."

(2) "When Christians meet someone in need, the most important thing they can do is listen. After that, it matters little whether they help the person."

(3) "When Christians meet people who are in need, they should first inquire about them, see if they are grateful people who will likely join the church, and then help them. If they are clearly not going to believe in Jesus, Christians should help someone else."

Put the three pieces of paper where the class members can read them; then lead a discussion about them. Ask for each statement: *Is this statement correct? Why or why not?*

F. Provide an opportunity for those who studied the church's healing ministry (either through a visit or by means of written materials) to report to the class. Show the class that, even though they may not think about it often, they are already involved in a healing ministry. Then ask if there are other ministries of healing—broadly construed—in which the church should be involved.

G. Close the session with a prayer that summarizes the conclusions you have reached and the commitments you have made.

Chapter 5: Commissioning [pages 53–64]

Preparation. Distribute the nametags you have made in a previous session, explain briefly the meaning of the tags, and ask those who have not been given tags if they wish to have one. Collect the nametags at the close of class.

A. Open the session with prayer; then have someone read today's passage aloud.

B. Encourage class members to focus for a moment on those who doubted. Summarize what the book says about doubt and disobedience [pages 54–55]. Then lead the class in exploring some issues related to doubt and despair.
1. Tell the group that a Christian Guatemalan poet, Julia Esquivel, has written a book entitled *Threatened With Resurrection* (Brethren Press, 1994). Her point there is that the Resurrection, in a sense, makes things more difficult for Christians by giving hope. Because there is hope, one cannot give up on the world but must continue to struggle. The Resurrection, therefore, is a kind of threat.
2. Invite members to close their eyes and imagine that they are the disciples. After three years of wandering and hoping, their hopes are now shattered. Deeply disappointed, they are getting ready to return home to their old lives and their old routines. Ask: *In such circumstances, would you be inclined to doubt or to have faith? Why?*
3. After class members have had a chance to respond, ask: *In what ways are we "threatened with Resurrection"? When do we doubt because to believe would launch us into risky and costly adventures?* Invite members to give examples if they wish.

C. Jesus commissioned those who doubted as well as those who worshiped him. The book suggests that being sent to make disciples may well be the best medicine for doubting disciples [page 57]. Ask: *Do you agree? Why or why not?* Invite group members to tell of experiences similar to what the book describes, of the author coming to greater faith in Christ by the very act of communicating the faith.

D. Now pose the opposite question: *Could it be that one reason our faith is not as deep as it should be is that we do not share it as we should?* Encourage group members to comment on this question.

E. Return to the nametags that people have been wearing, with the names given to them by the class. Point out that these names were given in recognition of some gift or characteristic the person had. In a way, what the group did when it gave its members these various names was to begin exploring what shape their Christian discipleship and ministry might take—or, in other words, they began exploring their possible commissioning. When Jesus gave Simon the name *Peter*, he was beginning to commission him for something. When we in this class named someone "Teach" or "Visitor" or "Doitright," we were pointing to some gifts or traits in that person, which might well lead to a particular form of service.
   1. Ask the class members what it has felt like, during these five weeks, to come to church on Sunday and be given this nametag with a strange name on it. Has it made them think about who they are and their place in the church? Has it given them ideas about things they should do or become? Do they now think that the name the group gave them was accurate? Are they proud of it? Have they lived up to it?
   2. Include yourself in this process, telling the class what the name they gave you has come to mean to you. (You may do this first, as a way to encourage others to do the same; or you may do it after the others have spoken.)

F. Tell the class that this exploration of names has made all of you see yourselves in a different light and that it may be calling you to places you have never been before. This can be frightening. (Remember that one can even be "threatened with resurrection.") The disciples would have had every reason to be frightened when

Jesus told them to go to "all nations." That is why Jesus began by telling them that he already had power over all the nations: "All authority in heaven and on earth is given to me." Wherever Jesus is sending us, he is already there waiting for us.

G. End the session with a prayer of dedication, asking God for guidance along the way of Christian service.

Chapter 6: Teaching [pages 65–73]

Preparation. Distribute the nametags you have made in a previous session, explain briefly the meaning of the tags, and ask those who have not been given tags if they wish to have one. Collect the nametags at the close of class.

Have a chalkboard and chalk or a large sheet of paper and a marker available.

A. Open the session with prayer, inviting the Holy Spirit to teach the class as you study today's passage from Matthew together.

B. Introduce the study with a general discussion of teaching and its authority. In that discussion, stress the following:

1. Our Scripture passage raises a profound question: What gives someone authority to teach? Ask: *What qualifications do you expect a teacher to have?* (Things such as "knowledge of the subject matter," "ability to teach," "respect for students," and so forth could be mentioned.) List the group's responses on a chalkboard or on a large sheet of paper.

2. In a traditional culture the main function of a teacher is to pass on the tradition. The society entrusts its upcoming generations to teachers who will socialize them into the mores and customs of the group as a whole. In such a society teachers, as depositories of the values and traditions of the community, are highly respected and are seldom controversial.

3. This function is disrupted when a teacher disagrees with some aspect of the tradition. At that point, there is a clash of authorities: that of the tradition versus whatever claim the teacher has for his or her own doctrines. (Mention the Scopes

trial of 1925, when a young teacher taught evolution and the community resented it.) Then the question is, Whose authority will prevail?

4. To some degree, this clash is what is going on in Jesus' teachings. As a rabbi he is supposed to uphold the tradition—and he does. But he interprets the tradition differently than do those who are officially in charge of that interpretation. The clash is inevitable.

C. Read aloud the Scripture passage (Matthew 21:23-27). After reading, invite class members to comment on how the question of authority plays a role in the passage.

D. Ask: ***Why do you think Jesus would not tell the religious officials by what authority he was teaching?*** (If he said it was from God, they would accuse him of blasphemy. If he said it was his own, they would simply silence him. If he said his authority was the same as God's, they would accuse him of the highest form of blasphemy.)

E. Engage the class in a discussion of the nature of Jesus' teaching authority. Ask: ***By what authority did Jesus teach?*** (Here you may summarize what the book says about "authority" and "authorship" [pages 66–68].)

F. Turn the attention of the class to our own teaching. Write the following propositions on a chalkboard or on a large piece of paper and ask the class to discuss whether each of the propositions is true and, if so, to what extent:

(1) "No matter whether we want to be or not, we are all teachers. Others see our example, hear our words, observe our lives."

(2) "As Christians, our teaching must both inform and form people. We must tell people things they did not know, and we must also invite them to become disciples of Jesus."

(3) "Our authority as Christian teachers is based on Jesus' authority. We are good teachers in the same measure that we teach as he did."

G. Provide opportunity for any who wish to do so to speak about an exceptional teacher who shaped their lives. Ask them what they would like to imitate in that teacher. Point out that all those teachers mentioned—like all good teachers—were also excellent learners. Then close the session with prayer, asking God to help class members become the best teachers they can be, both by continuing to learn and by teaching others.

Chapter 7: Witnessing [pages 74–84]

Preparation. Distribute the nametags you have made in a previous session, explain briefly the meaning of the tags, and ask those who have not been given tags if they wish to have one. Collect the nametags at the close of class.

Have a chalkboard and chalk or a large sheet of paper and a marker available.

A. Open the session with prayer; then have someone read aloud the passage of Scripture (Acts 1:6-8). Give the group a few moments to reflect on the passage.

B. Begin by asking: *What it is that the disciples expect when they ask if Jesus is about to "restore the kingdom to Israel"?* Point out that Jesus corrects them and that it is important to see where they were wrong and where they were right. Stress the following points:

1. The disciples *were right* in asking about the Kingdom. The "kingdom of God" is very important in both Mark and Luke, and Matthew speaks of the "kingdom of heaven." Explain that the two phrases mean exactly the same thing, for Matthew is simply using the Jewish custom at the time of speaking of "heaven" instead of referring directly to God. Underscore the point that according to the Gospels the kingdom or reign of God is central to Jesus' message.
2. The disciples *were wrong* in asking about the time. Read Jesus' response to their question and lead the class in a discussion clarifying this point.
3. The disciples *were also wrong* in limiting the Kingdom to Israel. Again, read Jesus' response and lead a discussion clarifying the point.
4. *Perhaps* (the text does not say so) the disciples were wrong in

thinking that the Kingdom would come with the same sort of power as common, everyday, earthly kingdoms. Invite group members to comment on this issue.

C. Having considered what was wrong with the disciples' question, have the group reflect on contemporary examples of those errors. Ask: *Do we ever make any of those errors? If so, in what ways?* As members respond, you may wish to help them think about the following, each of which relates to one of the disciples' errors:

1. Recently, there has been a spate of books and constant predictions about the end—how and when it will come.
2. Christians of a particular denomination or ethnic tradition sometimes have difficulty accepting others as Christians.
3. Many church members across the political spectrum hold to the notion that, if the church only had more political influence or more money or better organization, we could do more to bring about the Kingdom. Of course, these things may be good if used wisely; but if the church tries to wield "power" just as the world does, then it is as salt that has lost its flavor.

D. Ask class members to reflect on the differences between teaching and witnessing. Invite them to share their observations.

E. Write on a chalkboard or on a large piece of paper the two words "seeing" and "telling." Leaving aside for the moment the religious meaning of the term *witness*, point out that one cannot be a witness in a court of law without both "seeing" and "telling." Once you have clarified that double meaning of the word *witness*, ask: *How is it that a witness to Christ does each of the two (seeing and telling)?* At this point, follow the two-step outline provided in **Part I, Chapter 7, E.1–2** (page 30).

F. Ask the class to take a look at the "names" they have given one another, which they have been displaying on nametags through all these sessions.

1. Which of these names indicate that someone in the group is particularly gifted as a witness or is known for a particular energy in communicating the gospel?

2. Which of these names indicate gifts that, even though currently employed in other directions, could be useful in the task of witnessing?

3. What do the wearers of these names think of the group's observations?

G. Close the session with a prayer in which the class asks for the power of the Spirit in order to witness wherever members may be.

Chapter 8: Giving [pages 85–95]

Preparation. Distribute the nametags you have made in a previous session, explain briefly the meaning of the tags, and ask those who have not been given tags if they wish to have one.

Have a chalkboard and chalk or a large sheet of paper and a marker available, and place an offering plate at the front of your class setting.

A. Open the session with prayer, thanking God for the gift of the class members' time together.

B. Begin the study with a discussion of gifts people have received. In particular, ask members of the class what are some of the most valuable and meaningful gifts they have received from family, friends, or church members. Encourage people to consider not only material gifts but also gifts of time, wisdom, counsel, support, and so forth.

C. *When Christ Lives in Us* tells how a gift can be unwelcome [pages 86–88]. Ask the group to tell stories about unwelcome gifts in their own experience. As they share such stories, write on a chalkboard or on a large sheet of paper a word or two suggesting a reason why the gifts mentioned might not be welcome. (For instance, if someone tells of a person fighting alcoholism being given a case of champagne, write "callous." If someone tells of a man with a beard receiving shaving cream, write "useless.")

D. Ask: *When we say that the gift of Christ is sometimes unwelcome, what are our reasons? Look at the words on the chalkboard (or sheet of paper). Do any of them apply? Why or why not? Are there other reasons? What is required of those who accept the gift of Christ?*

E. The book suggests that giving involves more than money. Have the class explore that idea.

1. Ask the group to name nonmonetary gifts we can give and list each on a chalkboard or large sheet of paper. (Some examples include time; words or gestures of support; and knowledge, expertise, or abilities. Note that some of these may be on the name-tags of class members!) For each gift listed, ask: *What makes this gift valuable?*

2. Now turn the question around and ask the group to suggest ways in which we misuse, cheapen, waste, or exploit each of the gifts that have been listed.

F. The book points out that the greatest gift of Christ is Christ himself. He gave people food, health, wisdom, and many other things; but none of these things can compare with the gift of himself. Likewise, the greatest gift we can give is ourselves. And that greatest gift is also the least that God expects! Lead the class in a discussion of the following sentences from the book: "Paradoxically, receiving the Gift also means belonging to the Giver. He is ours, and we are his. These are two sides of the same coin; one cannot exist without the other. To claim the Gift, we have to give ourselves to him. There is no other way" [page 88]. Ask: *What does it mean to give ourselves to him? In what ways have we done that? As we come to the end of this study, are we ready to do it once more?*

G. At the close of this study, as a final act of giving yourselves, ask class members to remove their nametags and to hold them in their hands for a moment, reviewing what those names have come to mean. After a period of silence, when they are ready for it, ask the members to place these names on the offering plate at the front of your class setting. Then lead a prayer of thanksgiving for the greatest Gift, Jesus Christ.

Use in Four Sunday School Sessions (One Month)

The preceding material takes for granted that a Sunday school class will cover the book at the rate of a chapter a week and thus take eight weeks to complete the study. However, some classes may prefer to complete the study within a month (four sessions) or to extend it to a quarter (thirteen sessions).

If your class wishes to study the book in four sessions, the following is a suggested procedure: (Note: Check the **Preparation** section for each chapter above.)

FIRST SESSION: Chapters 1 (Calling) and 4 (Healing)

A. Follow instructions in **Part II, Chapter 1, A** (page 35).

B. Follow instructions in **Part II, Chapter 1, B** (page 35).

C. Point out that part of the reason the disciples are called is so that they may in turn call others (become fishers of people). When Christ calls us, he also calls us to call others.

D. Now turn to the Scripture lesson for Chapter 4 (Healing) and help the class enter into the story by following the steps outlined above, **Part I, Chapter 4, B-E** (pages 19–20).

E. Ask the class to list the similarities between the two stories (in both, Jesus calls someone; and in both, those persons' lives change). Show how this illustrates the point in Chapter 1, that when Christ calls, he also changes the one whom he calls. Close the session with a prayer that we may be responsive and faithful to our calling.

SECOND SESSION: Chapters 2 (Praying) and 3 (Feeding)

A. Follow instructions in **Part II, Chapter 2, A-D** (pages 37–38); but reduce or eliminate the roleplay under **C**.

B. From the instructions in **Part II, Chapter 3**, adapt **A-D**, skip **E**, and conclude with **F** and **G** (pages 39–40).

THIRD SESSION: Chapters 5 (Commissioning) and 7 (Witnessing)

A. Present Chapter 5 (Commissioning) by following the instructions in **Part I, Chapter 5, A-C** (pages 22–23).

B. Move directly to Chapter 7 (Witnessing). Present this chapter by doing the following:
   1. Read the Scripture lesson.
   2. Adapt the instructions for **Part I, Chapter 7, E-G** (page 30).

FOURTH SESSION: Chapters 6 (Teaching) and 8 (Giving)

A. Begin the session with the instructions for **Part I, Chapter 6, A-B** (pages 25–26).

B. Move directly to **Part I, Chapter 6, E** (page 27).

C. Read the Scripture passages for Chapter 8. Note that Jesus had authority for two reasons:
   1. As "author" he was in the form of God.
   2. Jesus had authority because he gave himself ("Therefore God also highly exalted him.").

D. Follow the instructions in **Part I, Chapter 8, B, F-G** (pages 31–33).

E. Close the session with a prayer of consecration and thanksgiving for the study.

Use in Thirteen Sunday School Sessions (One Quarter)

If the Sunday school class will study the book during an entire quarter, you will be able to spend two sessions each on five of the chapters and one session on each of the other three. The following distribution of time is suggested:

Sessions 1 and 2: Chapter 1 (Calling)
Session 3: Chapter 2 (Praying)
Session 4: Chapter 3 (Feeding)
Sessions 5 and 6: Chapter 4 (Healing)
Sessions 7 and 8: Chapter 5 (Commissioning)
Sessions 9 and 10: Chapter 6 (Teaching)
Sessions 11 and 12: Chapter 7 (Witnessing)
Session 13: Chapter 8 (Giving)

For the chapters to be studied in only one Sunday school session (Chapters 2, 3, and 8), follow the suggestions offered under **Part II** above. Those suggestions are made with a session of forty to fifty minutes in mind.

For the chapters to be studied in two Sunday school sessions (Chapters 1, 4, 5, 6, and 7), refer primarily to **Part I**, which is designed for sessions of up to two-and-a-half hours per chapter. It will probably be necessary to skip some of the steps or activities suggested there, since in a Sunday school setting you will have to begin the second session on each chapter by reviewing what was done in the first session. Also, do look at the points under **Part II**, where you may find some suggestions that you wish to follow. For instance, the suggestion of discussing possible new names and making nametags, which appears under **Part II, Chapter 1,** gives continuity to the entire study and leads to a final act of dedication; you may wish to take this into consideration.

Part III

Use in Retreat Settings

The book *When Christ Lives in Us* may be used by retreat groups in various ways. The first thing to be decided is whether participants will be expected to have read the book beforehand. If they have read the book, it will be possible to study it in its entirety during a weekend retreat. If they have not read it and will actually be seeing the book for the first time at the retreat, the limited amount of time available will not permit a careful study of the entire book. What follows are three options, depending on who the participants will be and on whether they will be expected to have read the book beforehand. (Naturally, a creative planning team or leader may combine elements from more than one option or decide on other approaches to the study of the book.)

Option A: Leadership Retreat

This option is particularly suited for a leadership retreat in which the participants will have read the book beforehand and will all be able to lead a group reflection.

1. Distribute the book among participants with sufficient time for all to read it before the retreat begins.

2. Divide the list of participants into groups of eight people. Distribute two copies of this Leader's Guide to each group.

3. Within each group, assign a chapter of the book to each person. He or she will be the leader of the session that covers that chapter. Following the suggestions given in **Part I and Part II** of this Leader's Guide, each participant will plan a study session on the specific chapter assigned to him or her.

4. During the retreat, have eight group sessions. The groups will study the various chapters in the order in which they appear in the book, with a different person leading the group each time.

5. Provide time for plenary sessions in which the entire group discusses what they have learned and/or decided. Also have a final worship service with an act of consecration.

Option B: Congregational Retreat

This option is particularly suited for a larger group—perhaps a congregational retreat or one with participants from more than one church. Again, it is expected that most participants will have read the book beforehand.

1. Distribute the book among participants with sufficient time for all to read it before the retreat begins.

2. Prepare a group of eight leaders, each of whom will be responsible for a particular chapter in the book. Distribute a copy of this Leader's Guide to each leader. Each leader will prepare a class session on the chapter that has been assigned to him or her, using the suggestions given in **Part I and Part II** of the Leader's Guide as modified by the retreat time frame. (It will be necessary for these leaders to meet before the retreat to make certain that what they plan fits together.)

3. Have eight rooms or meeting areas, each assigned to a particular leader and his or her chapter.

4. As participants arrive, divide them into eight groups.

5. During the retreat, have eight periods for group study.

6. Assign study groups to study leaders and chapters in "round-robin" fashion so that by the end of the retreat each group will have had opportunity to study all eight chapters and each leader will have met with all eight groups.

7. Provide time for plenary sessions in which the entire group discusses what they have learned and/or decided and for a final worship service with an act of consecration.

Option C: Weekend Retreat

This option is particularly suited for a retreat where it is not possible for participants to study the book beforehand. (The following design envisions a retreat beginning on a Friday evening and ending Sunday at noon. Adjustments may be made for other time frames.)

Before the Retreat

1. Make it clear that this will be a time for study, prayer, reflection, and spiritual growth. (Sometimes a "retreat" is a church outing,

55

designed more for fun and fellowship than for anything else. If some people come to this retreat with such expectations, they may be disappointed and may disrupt the rest of the group.)

2. Ask participants to bring a Bible and a notebook for keeping a journal (or have the participants bring the Bible and provide notebooks for them).

3. Make sure you have copies of *When Christ Lives in Us* for all participants.

Early Friday Evening: Opening Worship

Allow no more than one hour, preferably forty-five minutes.

Theme: Jesus Calls Us to Discipleship.

Scripture: Matthew 4:18-22.

You, the retreat leader, are to speak, having read Chapter 1 of the book. Emphasize the point that when Jesus calls us, he also changes us. The service should serve as an invitation to spend the rest of the weekend exploring Jesus' call to each one of us and what our response should be. Toward the end of the service (but still clearly as part of the service and not just as an announcement), give instructions for the remainder of the evening. Explain that each participant will receive a "Reflection Sheet" with a few simple but important questions. The participants are to spend the rest of the evening in study, prayer, and meditation, following the instructions on their Reflection Sheet and seeking guidance for the future. Encourage participants to read Chapter 1 of the book, which should aid them in understanding the scope of those questions on the Reflection Sheet. Let the group know how you will signal the end of this period of reflection and prayer. (It could be with a bell calling for closing prayers, followed by a bedtime snack.)

(If the group is able to be at the retreat location early enough, you may wish to have the opening service before supper and leave the entire evening for reflection and prayer. In that case, instruct the participants to read Chapter 1 of the book before beginning to deal with their Reflection Sheet.)

The Reflection Sheet should say:

Think about the following questions and write your reflections in your journal. Stop frequently for prayer, asking God's guidance in your responses.

(1) Whom Jesus calls, Jesus changes. How has Jesus changed my life?

(2) Sometime ago, Jesus called me to be a disciple. But Jesus is still calling me. Where is he calling me to go? What does he want me to do?

(3) Discipleship always involves leaving something behind ("traveling light"). What are some of the things I must leave if I am to respond positively to Jesus' call?

Saturday Morning: First Session

Allow approximately ninety minutes. This will be a plenary session with all participants meeting together for study and discussion under the direction of the retreat leader. Focus on Chapter 2 of the book, "Praying."

Ask participants to arrange their chairs so they have conversation groups of five or six persons each. They must all be able to hear what the leader says and also be able to enter into conversation with one another with a minimum of disruption.

1. Open the session with a prayer for illumination and follow with a hymn. [five to seven minutes]
2. Invite all to open their Bibles and read Luke 11:1-13. [two to three minutes]
3. Underscore the impact of the contrast between God's majesty (that God's name is to be hallowed) and the address of "Father." (See suggestions in **Part I, Chapter 2, D**, on page 13 of this Leader's Guide. Here, as elsewhere in these instructions, adapt the suggestions so that your questions are discussed in the small groups.) [ten to fifteen minutes]
4. While the participants are still assembled in small groups, turn to the parable in Luke 11:5-8. Point out that this is still part of the same lesson on prayer that Jesus is giving his disciples. Read the parable aloud. Analyze the parable as in the book [pages 27–29], calling the characters in the story "Friend A," "Friend B," and "Friend C." [five to seven minutes]
5. Now invite the small groups to consider the four situations described in **Part I, Chapter 2, F.1-4** (page 14 of this Leader's

Guide). After posing the question at the end of the first point, give the groups three or four minutes to respond; repeat the process for the other three points.

OR

6. A few days before the retreat, have three people with a creative and dramatic flair prepare the four skits suggested in **Part II, Chapter 2, C** (page 38 of this Leader's Guide). After each of these skits is presented, ask the groups to discuss how it relates to what we ought to pray for and why—as well as what we ought not to pray for and why. [twenty to twenty-five minutes for 5 or 6]

7. Continue with the suggestions in **Part II, Chapter 2, D** (page 38 in this Leader's Guide). If you did not do the skits, phrase the question in terms of the four situations you described and the participants discussed. [fifteen to twenty minutes]

8. Read the remaining verses of the Scripture passage (Luke 11:9-13). Then end with the suggestion that the highest gift, and the one we should constantly ask for, is the gift of the Holy Spirit—among other things, because the Spirit tells us what to pray for. [five to eight minutes]

9. Invite participants to spend the rest of the session praying in groups, asking for the gift of the Holy Spirit.

10. Close the session with a brief prayer.

Saturday Morning: Second Session

Allow approximately ninety minutes. This is to be a prayer session. Have participants gather in the small groups of the earlier morning session, in prearranged rooms or places, for joint prayer and reflection.

If the participants wish, they may talk about their journals and what they have written in them, about issues raised in the first morning session, or about other spiritual concerns. After thirty to forty-five minutes of sharing, they are to spend the rest of the session in prayer.

Saturday Afternoon

After lunch, provide two "Prayer and Reflection" periods of an hour each, with a thirty-minute break between. Mark the beginning and end of each period by ringing a bell or by some other means. Do not plan any structured activities for these periods. But do suggest that participants spend each of the two periods in a different one of the following activities:

(1) Private prayer

(2) Group prayer

(3) Reading some of the chapters of the book that will not be formally studied during the retreat

(4) Journal writing

(5) Seeking and/or giving spiritual advice

Saturday Evening: Plenary Session

Allow approximately ninety minutes. Focus on Chapter 7 of the book, "Witnessing." The session is to be led by the retreat leader (you), with seating arrangements as in the first session of the morning.

1. After an opening hymn and prayer, begin the session as suggested in **Part I, Chapter 7, B–C** (pages 28–29 in this Leader's Guide), adjusting those procedures to the different setting. Keep this discussion brief. [fifteen to twenty-five minutes total for these various points]

2. Continue with **Part I, Chapter 7, E** (page 30 in this Leader's Guide). Allow more time for this discussion, for it is at the heart of the matter. [twenty-five to thirty minutes]

3. Move to **Part I, Chapter 7, F** (for which you will have to study Chapter 5 of the book). Use this point as an invitation to all participants to witness to their faith. [five to ten minutes]

4. Point out that although usually when we speak of "witnessing" we mean doing so before unbelievers, there is also value in Christians witnessing to one another about what the Lord has meant to them. [three to five minutes]

5. Invite the small groups to spend the rest of the time in mutual testimony.

6. Dismiss the session with a brief prayer.

Sunday Morning: First Session

Allow for another unstructured period of one hour, similar to that on Saturday afternoon. Encourage participants to use this time in any of the activities suggested for Saturday and also in gathering their thoughts toward the end of the retreat.

Sunday Morning: Closing Worship

The session is to be planned and directed by the retreat leader and the planning team; it should last approximately one hour.

Theme: Jesus Commissions Us.

Scripture: Matthew 28:16-20.

You, the retreat leader, are to speak, having read Chapter 5 of the book. The emphasis is to be on the significance for our commission of the words of Jesus, "All authority in heaven and on earth has been given to me."

This should be a worship service with much participation on the part of all present. Allow time for testimonials, reports on what the retreat has meant to individual participants, requests for prayer, and so forth.

The worship service should conclude with a dramatic act of dedication, such as coming to the altar for prayer, placing one's retreat nametag on the altar, signing private pledges, and so forth.

Part IV

Use in Stewardship Studies

The book *When Christ Lives in Us* may be used as a tool to provide spiritual undergirding to a stewardship campaign. In order for this to occur to as great an extent as possible, everyone (and especially those actively involved in providing leadership for the stewardship campaign) should be encouraged to read the entire book as a devotional exercise. Make the book available to the congregation, and each Sunday during the campaign quote a few lines from it in the church bulletin. This could be coupled with two congregational Bible study sessions, one toward the beginning of the campaign and another toward the end. A good setting for these sessions could be a Wednesday night supper or similar event. The following is suggested for those sessions:

FIRST SESSION (early in the stewardship campaign)

This session combines Chapters 2 and 3 in the book ("Praying" and "Feeding"). Its purpose is to ground the management of our gifts and possessions in a life of prayer and devotion. Although participants will have been invited to read these chapters beforehand, do not take for granted that they have done so. Part of the purpose of the session is to show the congregation that this kind of reading and study can be exciting.

1. Distribute copies of the two passages, Luke 11:1-13 and John 6:1-14, to all participants. Every time you read a passage, invite the audience to follow your reading on their sheets.

2. Begin the presentation by reading aloud the parable in Luke 11:5-8. Summarize what the book says about this parable [pages 27–29]; then explain what you mean by "Friend A," "Friend B," and "Friend C."

3. Look at the four scenarios under **Part I, Chapter 2, F** (page 14 in this Leader's Guide). Describe each of those scenarios; then ask volunteers from the stewardship team seated around tables or in the various sections to discuss each of the scenarios in turn. (If the group is not too large, you may invite one or two comments from the floor after each of the four scenarios.)

61

4. Read aloud John 6:1-9. Point out that Jesus is now in the position of Friend B in the parable, with the crowd as Friend A.
5. List and explain some of the excuses Jesus could have given (as suggested in the book [pages 33–36]; see also **Part I, Chapter 3, B**, pages 16–17 in this Leader's Guide):
   a. The spiritual excuse
   b. The purity excuse
   c. The pragmatic excuse (not mentioned in the book)
6. Divide the larger group into thirds; then assign each smaller group to a particular excuse. Ask the members of each group to discuss if we ever use such excuses today and if we do, to think of examples. After three or four minutes of discussion, ask for a few examples so the entire group can hear them.
7. Read aloud John 6:10-14. Point out that Jesus, acting as Friend B, took what was available and prayed—that is, went to Friend C. The result is that the crowd (Friend A) could be fed.
8. Note also that:
   a. Jesus took what was available and used it. Friend B cannot go to Friend C without doing all he can to respond to the need of Friend A.
   b. Jesus gave thanks. Giving thanks for something means putting it at God's disposal. (See **Part I, Chapter 3, F.3**, page 18 in this Leader's Guide.)
9. Explain that during this stewardship campaign we will be exploring these questions:
   a. What are the needs of the world and the church (Friend A) that we are called to meet?
   b. What resources (in talents, time, expertise, money) do we have for responding to those needs?
   c. What are some of the ways we can "give thanks" for those resources—that is, put them at God's disposal?
10. Finish by reading the section in the book under the heading "Meanwhile" [pages 41-42]; then dismiss the congregation with prayer.

SECOND SESSION (toward the end of the campaign)

Base this session on Chapter 8 of the book, "Giving."

1. Before the session, distribute slips of paper with the following quote from the book: "Paradoxically, receiving the Gift also means belonging to the Giver. He is ours, and we are his. These are two sides of the same coin; one cannot exist without the other. To claim the Gift, we have to give ourselves to him. There is no other way" [page 88].

2. Begin the session by reading the passage from Philippians and commenting on Jesus the Giver and the Gift [see the book, pages 85–86].

3. Ask the groups around the tables or in the various sections to discuss the quote that was distributed. To what extent do they agree with the statement?

4. Explain that, as Wesley saw things, if we belong to Christ, we ought to (1) make all we can, (2) save all we can, and (3) give all we can [see the book, pages 91–92].

5. Another way of saying this is that Christians ought to have a "Giving Fitness Program," or "G.F.P." [Explain what the book says about the need to exercise the gift of giving, pages 91–94.]

6. Distribute "G.F.P. Worksheets," as described in this Leader's Guide (**Part I, Chapter 8, H**, page 33). Tell people that they are to take these sheets home, pray about them, discuss them with their families, fill them out, and keep them as a future measure of their "giving fitness."

7. Ask the groups around the tables or in the various sections to discuss what would be a reasonable measure of "giving fitness" for each of the items mentioned.

8. Invite the groups to pray for guidance as each member deals with the issues raised in those sheets and with what it means to accept the gift of Christ.

9. Close with a prayer giving thanks for Christ, God's great Gift to us.

Part V

Use in Membership Classes

The book *When Christ Lives in Us* may be used as part of the material for membership classes. The purpose would be to help new members understand how the Christian community understands itself and the sort of challenge it hopes to place before its members. In order to use the book in this way, two options are suggested:

Option A

Study the book as a group, in eight weekly sessions of an hour or two. Follow some of the suggestions listed in this Leader's Guide (under **Part I**, if they are two-hour sessions, and under **Part II**, if they are one-hour sessions). Taking into account that people in this group probably will not know one another as well as people in other groups, adapt the activities accordingly.

Option B

Ask participants in the membership class to use the book as part of their devotional discipline, reading a chapter a week, praying over what they read, and writing in a journal their responses to the following questions:

(1) What are some things I have learned in reading this chapter?
(2) What are some things I do not understand and would like to discuss when the group meets?
(3) What are some things I have decided I shall do?
(4) What are some things I think I must consider?

When the membership class meets for its regular weekly session, devote the first fifteen to twenty minutes to talking about the chapter that people have read. First, have them comment on what they have learned. Then, deal with the points they did not understand, either by discussing the chapter with them or by directing them to other resources. Encourage, but do not force, conversation on questions 3 and 4.